SCOTLAND
EAST & NORTH

ROGER SIVITER ARPS

Front cover: Just south of Montrose station are two viaducts which cross over the Montrose basin where it runs out into the North Sea. At around 7pm on the evening of Thursday 2 August 1990, Class 47/4 No 47635 *Jimmy Milne* runs over the southernmost of the two viaducts and heads for Aberdeen with the 17.00 train from Edinburgh.   *Roger Siviter*

Back cover: On Sunday 24 July 1988, English Electric Class 37/4 No 37421 waits to leave Thurso station (the most northerly point on BR) with the 11.22 service to Georgemas Junction, where it will join up with the 11.20 train from Wick, hauled by No 37414, to form the 11.46 service to Inverness. The Inverness train will be hauled by No 37414, No 37421 returning light to Thurso. On the right hand side can be seen the edge of the Highland Railway design wooden goods shed.   *Roger Siviter*

Right: Princes Street Gardens, to the west of Edinburgh Waverley station, is the setting as Class 27 No 27054 runs through this photogenic location with the 10.30 Dundee to Edinburgh train on 5 June 1986. At the rear of the train can be seen the Caledonian hotel, behind which was Princes Street station, which closed in 1965.   *Roger Siviter*

© Roger Siviter 2003
Published by Great Bear Publishing
34 Shannon Way, Evesham WR11 3FF Tel: 01386 765134

ISBN 0-9541150-2-3

Designed and produced by Viners Wood Associates Tel: 01452 812813
Printed in England by Ian Allan Ltd, Surrey.

Our journey starts at the Royal Border Bridge, just south of the ancient Border town of Berwick-on-Tweed. On the early morning of 17 April 1981, Peak Class 46 diesel No 46046 heads across the famous bridge with the first Edinburgh to Newcastle train of the day. Heading north is an unidentified Class 31 locomotive. The Class 46 locomotives were a final development of the Peak Class diesels, and were introduced in 1961.

Tom Heavyside

Introduction

Ever since the 1960s, when the ex-LNER A4 Pacifics used to work on the Glasgow-Aberdeen trains, I have been visiting Scotland to photograph the railways. For whatever the traction, be it steam (or industrial steam as at Waterside in Ayrshire) or diesel, together with its striking scenery and also a great deal of railway infrastructure, Scotland has much to offer the railway enthusiast. I can't claim to be Scottish, but my wife Christina can certainly claim to be half Scottish. Her father, a notable veterinary surgeon, Alexander ('Sandy') Mair came from Peterhead and studied at Aberdeen University, and so I would like to dedicate this book to his memory.

This book is a journey from the Border town of Berwick-on-Tweed to Wick and Thurso, both via the Highland main line from Perth to Inverness and also via the coast route over the Forth and Tay Bridges to Dundee and Aberdeen, and then inland to Inverness, from where we travel to the Kyle of Lochalsh, and then on to Wick and Thurso. The period is from the mid-1970s to the early 1990s, arguably the heyday of the locomotive-hauled trains.

I should like to thank all the following people for their help in compiling this book: Hugh Ballantyne, Tom Heavyside, Les Nixon, my wife Christina, and last but certainly not least all the railway men who made it possible.

Roger Siviter Evesham, 2003

Right, above: In days gone by, Berwick-on-Tweed was in Scotland but nowadays the actual Border is near Lamberton, just over two miles north of Berwick. Approaching the Border on Sunday 21 June 1987 is a smart looking Railfreight-liveried Class 26 No 26004 with a northbound electrification construction train. Electrification of this section of the East Coast Main Line (ECML) was in progress at the time, and within a few weeks of the date of this picture, gantries and catenary wires would be in place. *Roger Siviter*

Right, below: On 3 June 1979, English Electric Deltic Class No 55012 *Crepello* (named after the 1957 Derby winner) crosses the Border with the 08.00 Edinburgh to Kings Cross service. These photogenic locomotives were first introduced in 1961 to replace the former LNER Pacific locomotives on the East Coast Main Line between Kings Cross and Edinburgh. *Hugh Ballantyne*

For five miles between Berwick-on-Tweed and Burnmouth, the ECML skirts the North Sea coastline, making for attractive 'Railway Seascapes'. One of the popular and powerful Deltic locomotives No 55019 *Royal Highland Fusilier* is seen on the coast route just north of the Border with the 10.55 Kings Cross to Edinburgh train on 3 June 1978. No 55019 was preserved by the Deltic Preservation Society (one of five members of the Class to be saved) and now sees duty on main line charter trains.

Hugh Ballantyne

With only a few weeks to go before electrification of this stretch of the ECML, Class 47 No 47003 catches the late evening sunshine as it heads south near Burnmouth with a train of Cargowagons from Mossend Yard to Ripple Lane West on 31 July 1987.

Roger Siviter

English Electric Class 40 No 40068 is photographed near Burnmouth with an Edinburgh to York excursion train, on 3 June 1978. These Type 4 diesel locomotives were first introduced in 1958 and were withdrawn by 1988. However, several examples remain in preservation, and 2002 saw the return to main line charter workings of this famous Class in the shape of No D345. This locomotive is owned by the Class Forty Preservation Society, and is based at Bury on the East Lancashire Railway.

Hugh Ballantyne

After Burnmouth, the ECML runs inland for several miles through the attractive Border region around Houndwood and Granthouse. On 3 June 1978, Class 55 No 55016 *Gordon Highlander* rounds the reverse curves at Houndwood with the 08.00 Kings Cross to Edinburgh train. No 55016 is one of the five Deltics to be saved from the cutter's torch, and was preserved by the the D9000 Group at the Nene Valley Railway.

Hugh Ballantyne

Above: Class 37 No 37046 speeds through the site of Granthouse station with an up goods train at 6pm on the evening of Friday 31 July 1987. These English Electric Type 3 locomotives were first introduced on BR in 1960 and a few examples are still hard at work on the system today. Note the split headlamps, one of the front end variations on this Class of locomotive.   *Christina Siviter*

Opposite: In 1979, after the disaster at Penmanshiel tunnel, the tunnel was closed and the ECML and the A1 road were realigned to the west. Class 47/3 No 47324 is seen topping the 1 in 90 of Cockburnspath bank at Penmanshiel with an evening Mossend Yard to Ripple Lane West goods train on 27 May 1987. On the left hand side of the picture can be seen the A1 trunk road.   *Roger Siviter*

The clock tower of the North British Hotel at Edinburgh says that it is 12.30pm so the 12.10 Edinburgh to Kings Cross has to make up 20 minutes as it pulls out of Waverley station on 23 July 1974 with Deltic No 55020 *Nimbus* (named after the 1949 Derby winner) in charge. With its 3300hp (the most powerful on BR at the time) and an official top speed of 100mph, it should be able to regain the 20 minutes loss on its 393 mile journey to Kings Cross. No 55020 had the shortest life of any of the Class, entering service in February 1962, and being withdrawn in January 1980.

Hugh Ballantyne

On Sunday 6 April 1986, Class 27 No 27704 pulls out of Edinburgh Waverley station with the 13.20 train to Dundee via the Forth and Tay Bridges, a journey of 59¼ miles, taking some 98 minutes. Overlooking the scene is the stately looking North British Hotel with its elegant clock tower. *Roger Siviter*

Opposite: After leaving Waverley station, west and north bound trains pass through the Mound tunnel and then through Princes Street Gardens. Class 47/4 No 47613 *North Star* runs smoothly through Princes Street Gardens with the four-coach 11.20 Edinburgh to Dundee train. At the rear of the train can be seen the Mound tunnel, above which is the National Gallery. 6 April 1986. *Roger Siviter*

Right, above: We leave the Edinburgh to Dundee line at Saughton, and head for Perth and the Highland main line to Inverness via Stirling. Between Polmont Junction (where the Glasgow line leaves the line to Stirling) and Falkirk Grahamston is the junction for the freight-only line to the industrial complex at Grangemouth. About a mile south of the site of the former Grangemouth station is the old Grangemouth shed (65F) which is now a diesel depot. 'On shed' on 13 September 1987 are Class 26 No 26001 (outside shed) plus, left to right, No 26042, No 37118 and No 47313. *Hugh Ballantyne*

Right, below: Class 26 Type 2 diesel No 26040 waits to leave Stirling with a south bound goods train at mid-day on 1 August 1990. The Class 26 locomotives were first introduced in 1958, and were built by the Birmingham Railway Carriage and Wagon Co. (BRCW) at their Smethwick works. Note Stirling Middle signal box and the splendid bracket signal with Caledonian posts and finials. *Roger Siviter*

Looking a treat in its BR large-logo livery, complete with the Scottish Terrier and silver roof, is Class 47/4 No 47595 *Confederation of British Industry* as it pulls out of Stirling station on the afternoon of 31 March 1986 with the 10.30 Inverness to Euston – 'The Clansman' – a journey of 581$\frac{3}{4}$ miles, with arrival in Euston at 21.28.

Christina Siviter

Five miles north of Stirling and 41¾ miles from Edinburgh lies the ancient town of Dunblane, complete with a famous mediaeval cathedral, now greatly restored since Victorian times. Dunblane was also the former junction for the Caledonian line to Callander and Crianlarich, which closed in 1965 due to landslips. On the morning of 19 May 1978, Class 40 No 40060 approaches Dunblane station with an Edinburgh to Perth train. Like many of its contemporary diesel locomotive Classes, the Class 40s were given a nickname by enthusiasts. In this case they are known as 'Whistlers', which no doubt had something to do with the sound emitted by the six English Electric nose-suspended traction motors, especially when they were 'idling' in stations, etc. I well remember being just outside Blackpool North station on a September evening in 1983 and hearing this whistling noise, and on going into the platform area finding No 40155 on an arrival from Euston. *Tom Heavyside*

Gleneagles station is the setting as Class 27 No 27011 departs with the 11.38 Dundee to Glasgow train on 20 May 1978. On the left hand side of the station can be seen the platform and trackbed for the former branch line to Crieff, which closed on 6 July 1964. Note also the bow windows on the footbridge towers. This station is now a listed building. Just west of the station is the world famous (former LMS) Gleneagles Hotel and golf course. *Tom Heavyside*

Class 47/7 No 47704 *Dunedin* with the 15.25 Glasgow to Aberdeen (Dyce) service is seen near Dunning, north of Gleneagles, on 1 April 1986. The Class 47/7s were all fitted for 'Push-and-Pull' working, especially on the Glasgow to Edinburgh and Glasgow to Aberdeen routes. Note the attractive ScotRail livery of the locomotive and coaches, and the semaphore signal with Caledonian post and finial.

Christina Siviter

Two miles south of Perth is Hilton junction, where the line from Ladybank joins the line from Stirling. By kind permission of BR, I was able to photograph Class 47/4 No 47546 *Aviemore Centre* as it headed for Stirling and Glasgow with the 12.30 train from Inverness, on Friday 4 August 1989. At the rear of the train is Moncrieff (or Hilton) tunnel. Just to the east of this location, at Bridge of Earn on the Ladybank line, was the junction for the Glenfarg route to Edinburgh via Cowdenbeath.

Roger Siviter

A sunny scene at Perth as Class 26 No 26036 shunts empty coaching stock at the southern end of the station on 20 May 1978. This picture was taken from St. Leonard's bridge which, as I well remember from my 'steam bash' in the summer of 1966, had an entrance to the main up platform and so was ideal for photographers, but this has long since closed.

Tom Heavyside

Crossing the River Tay at Perth on 20 May 1978 is Class 40 No 40052 with the 15.30 Aberdeen to Glasgow train. The two styles of bridges make an interesting comparison, with the more modern metal bridge contrasting sharply with the elegant stone bridge built by Telford.

Tom Heavyside

The north bound 'Clansman' arrives at Perth's Victorian station on the evening of Tuesday 1 April 1986, hauled by Brush Type 4 Class 47/4 No 47636. This train left London Euston at 09.15 and is scheduled to arrive at Inverness at 19.55. On the other platform is a DMU forming the 17.20 stopping train to Edinburgh, and to the left of the unit are the Dundee line platforms.

Christina Siviter

Opposite: Our next location is the former Stanley Junction, some seven miles north of Perth, where the Caledonian route for Aberdeen via Forfar and the famous Kinnaber Junction leaves the Highland Railway route to Inverness. Although the line between Forfar and Kinnaber Junction closed in 1967, the 25 miles between Stanley Junction and Forfar remained open for freight traffic (until June 1982) as did Kinnaber Junction to Bridge of Dun and the branch line to Brechin, which closed earlier in 1981. Happily, however, the branch line from Bridge of Dun (just west of Kinnaber Junction) to Brechin is preserved and is now known as the Caledonian Railway (Brechin). This line is home to several Type 2 diesels, including Classes 25, 26 and 27. On 5 June 1982, the Angus Railway Group ran a 'Forfar Farewell' special from Perth to Forfar. The special, headed by Class 40 No 40143, is seen leaving the Forfar line at Stanley Junction and heading for Perth on the return journey. The Highland line is on the left hand side. *Les Nixon*

Right: With just a hint of sun, the first passenger train of the day from Inverness – the 07.00 to Glasgow – pulls out of Dunkeld station at 08.52 on Friday 4 August 1989, with Class 37/4 No 37419 in charge. The typical Highland Railway footbridge, signal box and semaphore signals all add to the 'railway atmosphere' of the scene. *Roger Siviter*

Left, above: Framed by a HR goods shed and signal box, Class 47/4 No 47518 pulls out of Pitlochry station on the afternoon of 3 August 1989 with the 14.22 Edinburgh to Inverness train. The resort town of Pitlochry is famous as a tourist centre for the Grampian region.
Roger Siviter

Left, below: On the afternoon of Sunday 3 October 1982, Sulzer Class 25 No 25059 and brake van are caught 'slumbering' in the small goods yard adjacent to Blair Atholl station, probably after working on a Sunday ballast works train. This view shows the attractive station buildings as well as the typical HR goods shed of wooden construction. The Type 2 Class 25 locomotives were first introduced in 1961 and lasted until the mid 1980s. They were nicknamed 'Rats' and several examples remain in preservation, including No 25059 (D5209) which was preserved on the Keighley and Worth Valley Railway.
Roger Siviter

Opposite: Two miles south of Druimuachdar summit (at 1484 feet, the highest railway summit in the British Isles) lies the long-closed station of Dalnaspidal. The platforms at this isolated station were staggered, the up platform being behind the photographer. The signal box has been closed for some time, but still looks in reasonable external order. Hurrying down the 1 in 78 of Druimuachdar bank on 2 June 1990 is Class 47/4 No 47550 *University of Dundee* with the 10.10 Inverness to Euston train, 'The Clansman'. Although it is early summer, snow still lies in the gullies.
Roger Siviter

Opposite: It is Sunday morning on 27 May 1990, and the still air around Druimuachdar is shattered by the sound of the exhaust from Brush Class 47/4 No 47636 *Sir John De Graeme* as it tops the summit of the 17 mile climb from Blair Atholl, and heads for the Highland capital of Inverness with the 22.00 sleeper from Euston, which also has limited seating accommodation. Arrival in Inverness is scheduled for 11.40.   *Roger Siviter*

Above: An Inverness to Mossend Yard freight train, hauled by Class 26 No 26027, is photographed south of Dalwhinnie on 11 April 1988. The snow-capped Cairngorm Mountains provide an attractive backcloth to this quintessentially Highland scene.   *Les Nixon*

As late as the summer of 1993, the English Electric Class 37s (or 'Growlers' as they are affectionately known) were still working passenger trains on the Highland main line to Inverness. No 37240 in 'Dutch' livery heads towards Dalwhinnie with the 13.33 from Glasgow to Inverness on Saturday 14 August 1993. The distance from Glasgow to Inverness via the Highland route is 180½ miles, and this particular train was allowed 3 hours 37 minutes for the journey, including 12 stops.

Roger Siviter

The broom is in full flower as Class 47/4 No 47635 *Jimmy Milne* pulls away from the attractive HR station at Dalwhinnie and heads south with the 16.33 Inverness to Edinburgh train on the 'glorious' 1 June 1990. In the distance above the locomotive can be seen the whisky distillery. Note also the semaphore signals and the signal box just visible above the footbridge. The ubiquitous Class 47s were first introduced in 1963, and built by either Brush Traction at Loughborough or BR Crewe Works. Their 'Indian summer' was 2002, mainly on cross-country trains to the West Country, but a few examples still remain in service. *Roger Siviter*

Opposite: With the Grampian hills and a brooding sky as a backdrop, Class 37/4 No 37419, in 'large logo' livery, catches the late afternoon sun as it heads past the Dalwhinnie distillery with the 13.33 Glasgow to Inverness train. 2 August 1989.

Roger Siviter

Above: Class 47/4 No 47630 emits plenty of exhaust as it pulls out of Kingussie station at 08.40 on 31 July 1990. The train is the 22.15 Euston to Inverness sleeper service. Kingussie is some twelve miles south of the ski resort of Aviemore, and is an ideal base for touring this picturesque area of Scotland.

Roger Siviter

Above: The 12.30 Inverness to Glasgow Queens Street, hauled by blue-liveried Class 47/4 No 47438, runs over Slochd viaduct on 4 April 1986. This attractive stone viaduct is situated just south of Slochd summit, roughly halfway between Carr Bridge and Tomatin. *Christina Siviter*

Opposite: The climb up to Slochd summit (as well as up to Druimuachdar) was hard going in steam days, often requiring double heading and banking locomotives on the heavier trains for the steep gradients around 1 in 60 to 1 in 80. However, Class 37/4 No 37428 *David Lloyd George* seems in no trouble at all as it tops the 1 in 60 at Slochd summit with the 11.25 Edinburgh to Inverness train, on 16 August 1993. The Railfreight livery of the locomotive well matches the ScotRail carriages. Note also the summit board, informing us that it is 1315 feet above sea level. *Roger Siviter*

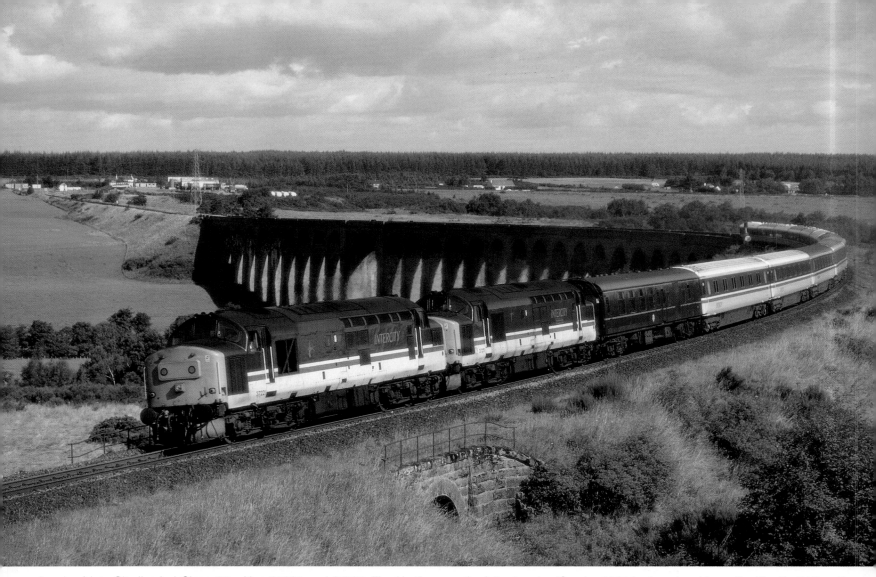

A pair of InterCity-liveried Class 37s, Nos 37221 and 37251 *The Northern Lights*, ease their way off the mighty 29-arch Culloden viaduct with the southbound 'Cock of the North' Scottish tour train, on Monday 16 August 1993. On the previous Saturday (14th) the train had visited the Kyle of Lochalsh, and the following day (Sunday 15th) had made a trip on the 'Far North' line. It was now headed for Aviemore and Perth. Culloden is, of course, the site of the famous battle in 1746 between Bonnie Prince Charles's Jacobite troops and the Government army. There is a Visitor's Centre at the site. *Roger Siviter*

Welshs Bridge signal box at Inverness is our next location, as No 37018 runs under the signal gantry with the 10.30 Inverness to Glasgow train, on 30 August 1986. At the rear of the train can be seen Inverness diesel depot. Within a mile to the east of this location is the junction where the Aberdeen and Aviemore/ Perth lines part. A few months after this picture was taken, re-signalling took place in the Inverness area, quickly making scenes like this become history.

Christina Siviter

We leave Inverness for the time being, and return to the outskirts of Edinburgh to take a trip to Aberdeen by the Forth and Tay Bridge route. At Dalmeny Junction, just south of the Forth Bridge, we see the diverted 1400 Glasgow to Edinburgh train as it heads away from the camera, with Class 27s No 27205 leading and No 27105 at the rear. On the right hand side is the normally freight-only line which leads to Winchburgh on the Edinburgh / Falkirk / Glasgow route, which on this day has been used for passenger diversion traffic, trains reversing at Dalmeny Junction. The Class 27 locomotives were first introduced in 1961, and were a development of the Class 26 diesels and, like the 26s, several examples remain in preservation. Sunday 21 May 1978. *Tom Heavyside*

Over the years, much has been written about the Forth Bridge, so let me just say that it was opened in 1890 and is arguably the greatest railway bridge ever built. Class 47/4 No 47633 leaves the northern portals of this magnificent tribute to Victorian engineering on the afternoon of 1 August 1990 with the 14.40 Edinburgh to Inverness service. Below the bridge nestles the small port of North Queensferry, where once passenger and car ferries plied their trade, before being made redundant in 1964 with the opening of the Forth road bridge.

Roger Siviter

With the Fifeshire town of Inverkeithing in the background, English Electric Class 20s Nos 20137 and 20156 have just crossed over the 550 feet long Jameson viaduct, and are heading for North Queensferry and the Forth Bridge with a mixed goods from Thornton to Millerhill Yard, 25 March 1991. The two mile climb from Inverkeithing to North Queensferry has a ruling gradient of 1 in 70, which in steam days often meant banking assistance for the heavier trains.

Les Nixon

Six miles south of Ladybank (the junction for the Perth and Dundee lines) lies Markinch, formerly the junction for the branch line to Leslie to the west. The branch closed in October 1967 (it had closed to passenger traffic in 1932) but a short two mile section remained open to service the Tullis Russel paper plant at Auchmuty. On 25 March 1991, Class 08 shunter No 08712 with a Thornton to Auchmuty freight trip working leaves Markinch station and takes the branch to Auchmuty, previously having run around its train at Markinch station. The English Electric Class 08s were one of the oldest diesel Classes on BR, being first introduced in 1952.

Les Nixon

Left, above: An eight-car DMU set leaves the two mile long Tay Bridge at Wormit (former junction for the line to Tayport) and heads south towards Ladybank on Sunday 19 April 1981. The remains of the line to Tayport, which closed in 1969, can be seen between the signal box and the DMU. Above the DMU can be seen the brick arches which lead to the northern end of the bridge. In the background is the city of Dundee, famous for many things, including the 'Dandy' and the 'Beano' comics, as well as in steam days the fine fleet of ex-LNER Class V2 2-6-2 locomotives at Dundee shed (62B). And so it was appropriate that in 1987, with the centenary of the opening of the bridge, V2 No 4771 *Green Arrow* ran on the special centenary shuttle train between Dundee and Wormit. *Roger Siviter*

Left, below: Dundee station (formerly Dundee Tay Bridge station) is the location as Class 26 No 26042 shunts the ECS of the 10.40 arrival from Edinburgh on 2 April 1986. Off the left of the picture was situated Dundee West station, which closed in 1965. *Roger Siviter*

Opposite: The sixteen members of the Class 47/7s were all fitted for 'Push-and-Pull' working, mainly between Edinburgh, Glasgow and Aberdeen. No 47703 *Saint Mungo* is seen at the rear of the 13.05 Aberdeen to Glasgow train as it approaches Arbroath station on 2 April 1986. Note the level crossing and adjacent signal box, and the fine looking factory building. *Christina Siviter*

A busy scene on the northern outskirts of Arbroath, as blue-and-yellow liveried HST No 43102 heads towards the station with the 14.00 Aberdeen-Edinburgh-Kings Cross train, arriving in London at 21.40. The trailer car is No 43076. On the left hand track is a Metro Cammell 3-car DMU waiting to enter Arbroath station with the 15.10 train to Dundee. Overlooking the scene is a magnificent stone built Victorian factory/warehouse, in sharp contrast to the modern factory building further on. 2 April 1986.

Christina Siviter

Passing the site of Inverkeilor station (which closed in the early 1960s), at around 8am on the morning of 2 August 1990, are a smart looking pair of Class 20 locomotives, Nos 20118 and 20137 *Murray B. Hofmeyr* with a north bound freight, probably from Dundee to Montrose. The Railfreight grey livery seems especially suited to the Class 20s. This Class was first introduced in 1957, and a few still remain in service. Several have been preserved, including No 20137 (D8137) on the Gloucestershire and Warwickshire Railway (GWR) at Toddington. Note also the North British signal box and more modern semaphore signals.

Roger Siviter

Left, above: Whilst waiting to photograph a train on the Forth Bridge (see picture on page 37) I got talking to a fellow photographer, who advised me that the 17.12 Dundee to Montrose local train and 18.08 return would sometimes have one of the Class 26 locomotives in charge. Sure enough, on the following evening (2 August 1990) No 26010 turned up, and is seen here crossing the southerly viaduct at Montrose with the outward working from Dundee. No 26010 (D5310) is one of several examples of this popular Class to be preserved.
Roger Siviter

Left, below: On the same day as the previous picture, and a couple of hours earlier, Class 47 No 47218 runs into Montrose station with a lightweight goods from Aberdeen. After a few shunting movements at the south end of the station, it will then leave for Dundee. Visible on the right hand side is the supermarket built on the site of the two-road engine shed, which was home to the former North British Class J37 0-6-0, which used to work the freight on the Brechin branch. This branch closed in 1981, but the line was preserved and is known as the Caledonian Railway (Brechin). Note the very high semaphore signal, and also Montrose North signal box.
Roger Siviter

Opposite: After the site of Kinnaber Junction (some three miles to the north of Montrose, where the old Caledonian route from Perth and Forfar joined the North British line from Montrose and Dundee, famous also in the 'Race to the North' in the 1890s) the line to Aberdeen runs through the site of Craigo station, which closed in 1956. However, at midday on 2 August 1990, there was still a smart looking Caledonian signal box at Craigo, as grey liveried Class 47/4 No 47422 speeds through with a mixed freight train from Aberdeen to Mossend Yard.
Roger Siviter

Opposite: On 13 July 1977, Class 25 No 25068 runs through the attractive Aberdeenshire scenery near Carmont, some 20 miles south of the 'Granite City', with an up evening postal train. As with the other Type 2 diesels (Class 24, 26, 27) several examples of these Sulzer Class 25s have been preserved, and can be seen at work on many of the preserved/heritage lines throughout the UK. *Tom Heavyside*

Above: Class 40 No 40142 pulls out of Aberdeen and passes under one of the famous signal gantries with an Aberdeen to Edinburgh train on the afternoon of 14 April 1979. In just over a couple of years of this date, re-signalling would make scenes like this a memory.
Les Nixon

Way out to East
Airport Terminal
and Heliport →

Over footbridge for
Airport Bus

Opposite: We now head north west out of Aberdeen on the line to Inverness. Our first location on this Great North of Scotland line is Dyce (former junction station for the line to Peterhead and Fraserburgh). This station is situated on the outskirts of Aberdeen, and nowadays is the 'junction' station for Dyce airport and heliport which, as well as other locations in the UK, serves the North Sea oilfields. A busy scene on Friday 21 August 1992, as Class 47/4 No 47674 enters Dyce station with the 09.16 Aberdeen to Inverness train, while Class 37 No 37015 waits to leave with an Inverness to Aberdeen freight train. The lines to Peterhead and Fraserburgh ran behind the impressive looking signal box. The Peterhead line (which closed in 1970) left the Fraserburgh line at Maud Junction. The Fraserburgh line closed in 1979. *Roger Siviter*

Right, above: 17 miles from Aberdeen is the small town of Inverurie, formerly home to the GNSR railway works, which closed in 1969. There was also a branch line to Old Meldrum to the north east of the town, which closed many years ago. Entering the station on 3 April 1986 is Class 37 No 37260 *Radio Highland* with the 10.32 Inverness to Aberdeen train. The splendid footbridge and station buildings are all worthy of note. *Christina Siviter*

Right, below: This picture was taken a few minutes before the previous scene, and shows a pair of blue-liveried Class 20 locomotives, Nos 20114 and 20123, pulling through Inverurie station with an east bound timber train. Beyond the station footbridge can be seen the GNSR signal box. Apart from a short distance around Kennethmont, the line is single track throughout, with passing points at stations. On this occasion, the freight was held at Inverurie until the arrival of the 11.40 Aberdeen-Inverness train, hauled by Class 47 No 47049. Note that both east and west bound trains use the west bound platform at this station. *Christina Siviter*

Our old friend (see picture on page 49 top) Class 37 No 37260 *Radio Highland* enters the attractive station at Insch with the 12.00 Inverness to Aberdeen train, 8 August 1988. There is much to see in this picture, from the waiting room and the base of the water tower on the left hand side to the splendid looking Great North of Scotland signal box of wooden construction. As can be seen, this part of Aberdeenshire is mainly farming land, and Insch is one of several very pleasant small towns in the area.

Christina Siviter

Class 47/4 No 47643 is photographed to the west of Insch with the 10.38 Inverness to Aberdeen service on 8 August 1988. In the background is Wishach Hill – 1375 feet high. *Christina Siviter*

Above: This next picture was also taken on Monday 8 August 1988, only this time in the mid afternoon. The location is the long-closed station of Kennethmont, which is situated 31 miles from Aberdeen and 8 miles from Huntly. Railfreight-liveried Class 37 No 37196 speeds through the old station with an Aberdeen to Inverness freight working. Part of the station building can be seen on the right hand side, and to the right of the signal box is the station name board. Note also the double track. Out of sight behind the photographer is a large distillery.

Christina Siviter

Opposite: After the double track section through Kennethmont, the line reverts to single track at Leith Hall (a mile or so to the west of Kennethmont) where, on the evening of 30 May 1990, Class 47/4 No 47460 rounds the tight curves as it heads for Aberdeen with the 17.02 train from Inverness. The four coach train must seem a very light load for this Type 4 locomotive.

Roger Siviter

Some five miles south of the market town of Huntly is the small village of Cults.The late evening sun highlights No 47641 *Fife Region* as it hurries past this small farming community with the 18.10 Aberdeen to Inverness train on 27 May 1990.

Roger Siviter

On 7 September 1982, Class 26 No 26029 crosses the two-arch Huntly viaduct as it approaches the town of the same name with an afternoon Aberdeen to Inverness train. At this time, the Type 2 Class 26 locomotives were regularly seen on passenger duties on this route as well as on some freight workings, including the whisky train from Keith to Aberdeen. *Les Nixon*

Above: Framed by semaphore signals, Class 47/7 No 47717 approaches Huntly station at 7.30am on the morning of 28 May 1990 with the 06.33 train from Aberdeen to Inverness. The train is due to arrive in the Highland capital at 08.54, having been allowed 2 hours 21 minutes for the 108¼ mile journey, which also includes eight stops. *Roger Siviter*

Opposite: This area of north eastern Scotland, roughly between Aberdeen and Inverness, was once a maze of lines, no more so than around Keith and Elgin where, in pre-grouping days, the Highland Railway and the Great North of Scotland competed for traffic. On 27 July 1992, Class 47/4 No 47677 *University of Stirling* approaches the old junction station of Keith with the 09.16 Aberdeen to Inverness service. Keith once boasted a small loco shed (which was located

just behind the photographer) and was the junction for the HR line to Inverness, which is part of today's through route, as well as a HR branch to Portessie on the north coast which connected with the GN of S coast route from Elgin. Also at Keith was the GN of S line to Craigellachie, which was the junction for the Elgin and Boat of Garten lines. This last route was closed in the 1960s with the exception of the section from Keith to Dufftown, which was used for freight traffic and excursions. This section was due to be closed, but happily has now been preserved and is known as the Keith and Dufftown Railway, with trains running between April and September and also in December. Also preserved is the line from Boat of Garten to Aviemore. This is known as the Strathspey Railway.

Roger Siviter

Opposite: Boat o' Brig, eight miles west of Keith, is where the line crosses over the River Spey and then heads north westwards for the next ten miles to Elgin. The 15.24 service from Aberdeen to Inverness has just crossed over the River Spey and is heading for Elgin with Class 37 No 37025 and Class 47/4 No 47674 *Women's Royal Voluntary Service* in charge. At this point, the train was some 90 minutes late, so perhaps the double heading was due to locomotive failure. The locomotive liveries make an attractive contrast. 31 July 1992. *Roger Siviter*

Above: Elgin once boasted two stations (HR and GN of S) and also a small locomotive shed. Today there is just the one station (HR) but there is still a goods yard, known as Elgin East Goods. On the afternoon of 9 August 1988, Class 37/4 No 37418 *An Comunn Gaidhealach* pulls out of the yard with a mixed goods bound for Inverness. In the background can be seen timber wagons which at the time formed a fair amount of the freight traffic in the area. (See lower picture on page 49) *Christina Siviter*

Opposite: These next two pictures (by kind permission of BR) well illustrate tablet exchange on this single line route. The first scene, taken on 20 August 1983, shows the signalman at Elgin (west box) about to pass the token to the crew of Class 47 No 47118 as it approaches with the 13.55 Aberdeen to Inverness train. The second scene shows the token exchange at Forres (east box) on 22 August 1992. The train is the 09.16 service from Aberdeen to Inverness, hauled by Class 37 No 37251 and Class 47/4 No 47677 (just visible behind the signalman). On the left hand side are the token exchange steps for east bound trains. Also note that Forres was the junction for the HR line to Boat of Garten and Aviemore.   Left: *Christina Siviter*. Right: *Roger Siviter*

Above: The popular seaside resort of Nairn is our next location, as Class 37 No 37251 enters the station with the 12.15 Inverness to Aberdeen train on Saturday 22 August 1992. On the right hand side is Nairn West box where, after resetting the signals and points, the only signalman would then cycle down to the east signal box to repeat the procedure after the train's departure, and obviously vice versa for west bound trains.   *Roger Siviter*

Above: A smart looking Class 37/4 No 37419, complete with Highland Rail motif on the cabside, waits to leave one of the Far North/Kyle line platforms at Inverness station on the evening of 29 August 1986 with the 17.55 to Kyle of Lochalsh train. At the rear of the train is the overall roof, which also covers part of the Perth/Aberdeen platforms. Note also the delightful HR station frame box, behind which is the stock of the 17.55 departure to Aberdeen.   *Roger Siviter*

Opposite: This next picture, also taken on 29 August 1986, shows Inverness Rose Street signal box, to the left of which is Inverness diesel depot. In the foreground is the avoiding line, which connects the Perth/Aberdeen lines with the Kyle/Far North routes. Beyond and to the right of the box can be seen Class 37/4 No 37418 waiting to leave on the 17.35 service to Wick and Thurso.
Roger Siviter

Turning round from the previous scene, we see No 37418 as it approaches Inverness on 30 August 1986 with the 06.00 from Wick and Thurso, arriving in Inverness at 10.10. Note the beautiful bracket signal with HR posts and finials. Also, at the rear of the train can be seen the start of the old bridge over the River Ness, which a storm washed away on 7 February 1989, leaving several Class 37s marooned on the Dingwall side. The following year, a new replacement bridge was opened.

Christina Siviter

On Sunday afternoon, the 21 August 1983, Class 37 No 37262 approaches Clachnaharry signal box for token exchange prior to crossing over the Caledonian Canal with the 14.10 from Kyle of Lochalsh to Inverness. The Caledonian Canal runs from just north of Inverness through Loch Ness and on to Fort William, a distance of around 70 miles. *Christina Siviter*

Above: In their last regular year of working on the Kyle of Lochalsh line, Class 37/4 No 37404 *Ben Cruachan* in InterCity livery threads the attractive countryside just south of Dingwall, and heads for Inverness with the 10.30 Kyle to Inverness train on Sunday 15 August 1993. Note the green and cream liveried excursion coaching stock, specially for use on the Kyle route. *Roger Siviter*

Opposite: Just north of Dingwall the two routes separate, with the line to Wick and Thurso heading north and the Kyle line swinging to the west. No 37415 is pictured just west of Achnasheen (some 46 miles from Inverness and 36 from Kyle) with the 15.28 train from Kyle to Dingwall on 1 August 1989. These trains (and the Wick and Thurso trains) all terminated and started at Dingwall, due to the collapse of the bridge over the River Ness at Inverness the previous February. *Roger Siviter*

Above: As the line approaches the Kyle of Lochalsh, it runs by the side of Loch Carron. At Fernaig (some 8 miles from Kyle) we see No 37415 again, only this time on the 11.10 Inverness to Kyle, on 23 July 1988. In the background is Loch Carron, overlooked by the North Strome Forest and the adjacent hills.

Roger Siviter

Opposite: A mile or so west of the previous picture, inside the grounds of the Highland Farm animal sanctuary, we see Class 37/4 No 37417 *Highland Region* as it heads east through beautiful Highland scenery with the 15.28 Kyle to Dingwall train, on 31 July 1989.

Roger Siviter

At Erbusaig, some three miles from the terminus at Kyle, the line runs by Erbusaig Bay. On the evening of 30 July 1989, Class 37 No 37415 glints in the late sunlight as it rounds Erbusaig Bay with the 16.22 Dingwall to Kyle of Lochalsh train.

Roger Siviter

On the afternoon of 27 July 1989, Class 37/4 No 37421 pulls out of the Highland Railway terminus at Kyle of Lochalsh with the 15.28 train to Dingwall. In the other platform beyond the wall can be seen the stock of the 17.00 train to Dingwall. Overlooking the scene are the magnificent hills of the Isle of Skye.

Roger Siviter

We leave the Kyle route and join the Wick and Thurso line at the junction just north of Dingwall station where, on Saturday 20 August 1983, Class 26s Nos 26035 and 26024 take the token and head north for Wick and Thurso with the 11.40 train from Inverness. In a short distance. the Kyle line swings away to the left. Scenes like this have long disappeared with the advent of radio signalling in the area. Note the signalman's cabin behind the bushes.

Christina Siviter

The Cromarty Firth and the Black Isle make an attractive backcloth as Class 26 No 26032 enters Invergordon station on 12 July 1984 with the 11.35 Inverness to Wick and Thurso train. There is much to enjoy in this HR scene, from the signal box and goods shed on the right to the station with its fine building and footbridge. And of course, the Post Office van complements the scene.

Tom Heavyside

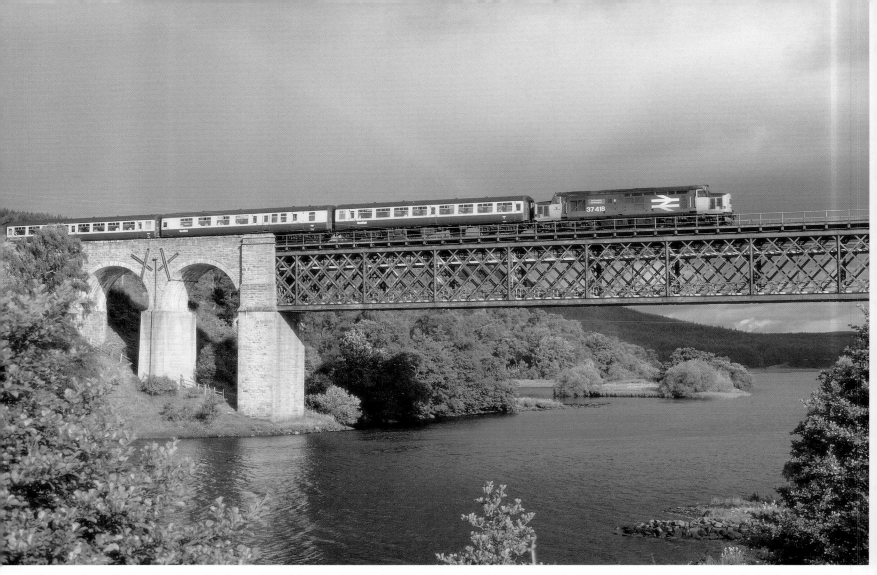

A few miles after Invergordon, the line swings inland to the north west and follows Dornoch Firth until it crosses over the Kyle of Sutherland at Invershin, some 61 miles from Inverness. On 25 July 1988, No 37418 *An Comunn Gaidhealach* crosses over Invershin Bridge with the 06.35 Inverness to Wick and Thurso train. There are stations at both ends of the bridge, Culrain to the south and Invershin to the north, and they are around half a mile apart. I was fortunate with the weather which produced this rainbow. *Roger Siviter*

On leaving Invershin, the line runs eight miles north to Lairg and then turns eastward, passing the site of The Mound station, formerly the junction for the branch line to the attractive resort town of Dornoch, which in its latter days was worked by GWR 0-6-0 pannier tanks. After The Mound, the line runs north eastward, roughly by the side of the North Sea. At Portgower, just south of Helmsdale, Class 37/4 No 37415 heads south on the afternoon of 4 April 1989 with the 12.38 Georgemas Junction (12.12 ex Wick, 12.14 ex Thurso) to Dingwall.

Christina Siviter

Opposite: After Helmsdale, the line runs inland through the Strath of Kildonan, and then runs easterly to BR's most northern junction at Georgemas. On the same day as the previous picture (4 April 1989) No 37415 approaches the outlying station of Scotscalder, some four miles west of Georgemas Junction, with the 07.06 train from Dingwall to Wick and Thurso. Ben Dorrery makes an impressive backdrop.   *Christina Siviter*

Above: An interesting scene at Georgemas Junction (some 147¼ miles from Inverness) on 2 June 1977. Class 26 No 26022 pulls out of the junction station with the 12.03 train to Inverness, which departed from Wick with No 26022 in charge at 11.41. At the rear of the train can be seen No 26021, which earlier had brought in the 11.43 from Thurso, which then joined the rear of the Wick train to form the 12.03 service to Inverness. After the departure of this train, No 26021 will then work the Thurso portion of the morning freight, seen on the left hand side of the picture on the Thurso line. The signal box and semaphore signals complete the picture.   *Les Nixon*

Class 37/4 No 37421 coasts into Georgemas Junction station on the afternoon of 3 April 1989 with the 12.06 train from Dingwall to Wick and Thurso. This view shows well the HR station house and footbridge. The line to Thurso can just be seen between the coaches and the footbridge. In a few minutes the train will split, with the first carriages going forward to Wick hauled by No 37421, and the rear portion travelling the 6¾ miles to Thurso, hauled by Class 37/4 No 37415. At the end of the siding can be seen the shed which houses the line's snow blower, essential for the winters in this part of the world. A comparison with the previous picture shows that this shed is a fairly new addition. Note also the snow barrier.

Roger Siviter

The 12.12 train from Wick approaches Georgemas Junction, hauled by Class 37/4 No 37417 *Highland Region*. After joining up with the 12.14 from Thurso, this will then go forward as the 12.29 Georgemas to Dingwall (hauled by No 37417). 3 April 1989.

Roger Siviter

14 miles east from Georgemas is the port of Wick, and like the port of Thurso it is also a convenient stop-over for tourists to John o' Groats. Whereas Thurso is the port for the ferries to the Orkneys, Wick can boast an airport for, amongst other things, the same services. On 3 April 1989, No 37421 is seen at the attractive station at Wick with the 18.12 to Dingwall train, having worked in earlier with the 12.06 from Dingwall (see picture on page 78). *Roger Siviter*